The Wonder of Nature in Rhythm & Rhyme

Melody Hamby Goss

Illustrator: Gerd Annie Nystrom

To order additional copies of this book, contact:
Xlibris
1-888-795-4274
www.Xlibris.com
Orders@Xlibris.com

The
Wonder of Nature in Rhythm & Rhyme

About the Illustrator

Gerd Annie Nystroem is an artist, photographer, animal advocate and environmentalist.

She was born in the north of Norway, growing up in the capitol city of Oslo. As a child, she and her family spent many happy times and every holiday in the mountains where they had a cabin.

The love and passion she feels for the wildness of nature, the beauty of her surroundings has endured into adulthood when she began painting.

A studio in her home allows for freedom of spirit, where the winters keep her homebound much of the time. Painting her beloved wildlife by the embers glow of her woodstove has allowed her works to come to life on a canvas soon to become one of her living memories.

Visit Gerd's Facebook page "Gerds Animal Paintings" to walk through a tapestry of beautiful animal and wilderness paintings.

This book is dedicated to everyone, anywhere caring about our planet, environment and wildlife…

"There may be days when I can't help an animal in need, but the day will never come that I won't try"…

Paul Oxton

Today is tomorrow's memory…

Wonders of Nature in Rhythm & Rhyme

The songs of the birds are the ballad of the forest. And while we still might have the forest without the songs, we would have lost the story. Therefore, at the point we lose our song we have likewise lost our story...

Craig D. Lounsbrough

"Asleep the Fairies"

All forest are one…they are the echoes of the first forest that gave birth to Mystery when the world began…
-Charles de Lint Spiritwalk

Faint the stars in twilight's glance,
On forest, floor bright moonbeams dance…
Haunting meadows therefore still,
Yet waiting songs of
Whippoorwills…

Silent there the fairies sleep,
Like echo's cry in winter's deep…
Mountains reach to touch the sky,
Faint the stars as twilight
Dies…

Fields and woodlands soft and bright,
Brambles bloom in gay delight…
Cradled there untouched nor seen,
Fairies sleep in forest
Green…

Weeps the wolf and eagles there,
Coyotes cry with grizzly bear…
Untouched green forest left to grow,
As meadows wait for
Winter's snow…

Asleep the fairies dream unseen,
Dreaming of their forest
Green…

As my eyes search the prairie I feel the summer in the `spring…

Chippewa Song

"Awaits the Winter"

She turned to the sunlight and shook her yellow head, and whispered to her neighbor; "Winter is dead"...
-A.A. Milne

There in hiding winter waits,
As forgotten glories fade...
Twirling leaves on ground they fall,
From woodland, hills
And glades...

Birds of song no more we hear,
In silence autumn creeps...
Gone sweet summer gentle heart,
Lapsed again in
Sleep...

Hides the sky in cloudy gray,
As last of leaves they die...
Deep they cover woodland floor,
When winters saunter
By...

Springtime alas! With blush admired,
Waste not her time for me...
As glories fade in hills and dales,
Green again and fair
Is she...

I heard a bird sing in the dark of December. A magical thing and sweet to remember. We are nearer to spring than we were in September...I heard a bird sing in the dark of December...

Oliver Herford

"Bare of Green Attire"

Because the birdsong might be pretty, but it's not for you they sing…and if
you think my winter is too cold, you don't deserve my spring…
-Erin Hanson

Feathers cold the robin asked, "Where is spring my friend"?
With little pride, a tiny bud hides from winter's wind…
"Not here, not here" cries out a tree bare of green attire,
Woodland's host this mighty Oak robins
Most admire…

Cottonwoods and birches white there by rivers bend,
Mingled there by woodland's host hiding from the wind…
Upon a hill tulips peek nodding to the cold,
Mo more we fear the winter's breeze,
Snubbing winter's hold…

Distant warblers robin's friends sing from junipers,
As tiny tulips slowly peek whenever springtime stirs…
Sleeping yet the buds of May snuggled in their bed,
Despair of tulips peeking there, yellow
Blue and red…

Faded winter springtime's foe, victor garb of woe,
Scattered there with little pride winter
Turns and goes…

6

To see a World in a grain of sand and a heaven in a wild flower. Hold infinity in the palm of your hand and eternity in an hour…

William Blake

"BENEATH QUEEN-MOON"

The moment you doubt whether you can fly, you cease forever to be able to do it…
-Peter Pan

Listen there and you shall hear,
Music in the vales…
A rustle soft from fairy wings.
Spinning fairy
Tales…

Beneath Queen-Moon they cluster still,
As playful sprites and fays…
Flowers there unfurled with scent,
Secret yet their fairy
Ways…

Adieu the day in twilight fades,
As tolls each midnight hour…
Rustles then soft fairy wings,
Scenting sweet their
Flowers…

Beneath Queen-Moon in dark of night,
While spinning fairy-tales…
Moonbeam sparkled fairy wings,
Flutter through the
Vales…

...so I return to the ocean depths where swimming creatures fly. For there I can soar with the whales and fish that daily touch the sky...

Richelle E. Goodrich

"By Ocean Dunes"

Hark, now hear the sailors cry, smell the sea, and feel the sky, let your soul & spirit fly, into the mystic...
-Van Morrison Into the mystic

On coral tinted shores of sea,
Voiceless words from shells to me...
Centuries still'd forever sigh,
By ocean dunes that
Never cry...

Enchanted reefs of coral there,
A sunless crypt as mermaid's lair...
Where herons wade and egrets fly,
By ocean dunes that
Never cry...

Voiceless words as trade winds blow,
Of tales untold the story goes...
Yo-ho-ho old pirates sigh,
By ocean dunes that
Never cry...

Cypress trees in ghostly calm,
Wink knowingly to greening palm...
Awaiting death 'neath bluing sky,
By ocean dunes that
Never cry...

Voiceless words from shells to me,
On coral-tinted shores of sea...
Hidden gators there defy,
By ocean dunes that
Never cry...

Pirates old in disbelief,
Of centuries past by coral reef...
Guard yet the gold of Captain Bly,
By ocean dunes that
Never cry...

Yo-ho-ho the pirates boast,
On coral-tinted ocean coast...
Wooden-legged without an eye,
By ocean dunes that
Never cry...

Guard still the gold of Captain Bly,
By ocean dunes that
Never cry...

G.A. NYSTN

Elvish singing is not a thing to miss, in June under the stars, not if you care for such things…

J.R.R. Tolkien

11

"Dancing in the Mist"

I have been in the land of the Faerie for years and it is a place where mortal blood is turned to fire. It is a place of beauty and terror beyond what can be imagined here. I have ridden with the Wild Hunt. I have carved a clear path of freedom among the stars and outrun the wind. And no I am asked to walk upon the earth again…

-Cassandra Claire

Wicked they in meadows dance,
As specter'd elves with ghostly lance…
Forest fey as fairies may,
Chance to see some ill
Of me…

Among the woods their chanting song,
In mist, they dance to mortals wrong…
As they sing this chanting thing,
Forevermore the ravens
Wing…

Away, away a wolf'n howl,
As specter'd elves with ghostly scowls…
In mist they dance to mortals wrong,
As forest fey I now
Belong…

Adorn me not with song or rhymes,
As mortal once in other
Times…

12

I have come to terms with the future. From this day onward I will walk easy on the earth. Plant trees, kill no living things. Live in harmony with all creatures. I will restore the earth where I am. Use no more of its resources than I need...and listen, listen to what it is telling me...

Earth Prayers

"Far Beyond the Waterfall"

For us, the world was full of beauty; for the other it was a place to be endured until he went to another
world…but we were wise. We knew that a man's heart, away from nature becomes hard…
-Chief Luther Standing Bear

Grandmother moon alone she weeps,
No creatures there in forest sleep…
Howls of wolf with eagles song,
In fields and woods no more
Belong…

Falling leaves on forest floor,
In solitude she knew before…
Far beyond the waterfall,
The echoed cry of
Creatures all…

Deer white-tailed and foxes red,
In laurel thicket long since dead…
Scenting not the midnight hour,
Forever gone the Lemon
Flower…

Far beyond the waterfall,
Grandmother moon and angels all…
Weeps alone in silence there,
At woodlands dead and
Meadows bare…

Howls of wolf with eagles song,
In fields and woods no more
Belong…

It is time we all stand together, to be the voice of the voiceless before it's too late...extinction means forever...

Paul Oxton

"FOREST KINGS"

I find my soul in a forest…
-Kdear dhepe

Howl the wolf in woodlands freeze,
Windswept the cold this winter's eve…
As whisper, soft speaks evergreens,
When prowls the wolves as
Forest kings…

Bare of leaves old oak'n trees,
Bends not to winter's angry breeze…
Sparrows there on limbs unseen,
When prowls the wolves as
Forest kings…

Echoes not their faded howls,
When yesterday the wolves once prowled…
Fall of snow in woodland's seen,
When prowls the wolves as
Forest kings…

Away! Away! Where spirits sleep,
In fall of snow in woodland's deep…
Forlorn the forests' evergreen,
When prowls the wolves as
Forest kings…

In fall of snow I bid adieu',
To echoed howls once I knew….
Unseen the sparrows on the wing,
Once prowled with wolves as
Forest Kings…

In a few blinks, you can almost see the winter fairies moving in...but first, you hear the crackle of their wings...

Vera Nazarian

"Kings in Traces"

I wonder if the snow loves the trees and fields, that it kisses them so gently? And then it covers them up snug, you know, with a white quilt; and perhaps it says, "Go to sleep, darlings, till the summer comes again...
-Lewis Carroll

Half-dream was I when whispered bells,
At twilight heard in snowy dales...
Flakes of snow in silence dance,
O'er woodland's path as
Horses prance...

Covered they the branches bare,
Grieve for spring in winter's air...
Awake am I as horses neigh,
Kings in traces dappled
Gray...

White the flakes this winter's nigh,
As diamonds sparkle from the sky...
Woodlands bare their echoes greet,
The whispered sound of
Horses' feet...

O'er woodland's path the dappled grays,
My house they pass to my dismay...
As kings in traces prancing by,
As sleigh bells ring this
Winter nigh...

Asleep I dream by fires glow,
Of whispered bells in
Winter's snow...

Shed no tear! Oh, shed no tear! The flower will bloom another year. Dry your eyes! Oh dry your eyes! For I was taught in paradise to ease my breast of melodies – shed no tear...Fairy Song....

John Keats

"ON FAIRY LIGHT"

Don't you know that everybody's got a fairyland of their own?...
-P.L. Travers

Immortal light of moon forlorn,
Dreams fair the maid her wishes born…
There amid the sapphire night,
Tomorrow bound on
Fairy light…

Sandaled feet 'neath satin gown,
Tightly held a tarnished crown…
Beyond the moon as fairies fly,
Sweet maiden weeps when
Dreamers die…

Immortal light on tarnished crown,
Saddened eyes casting down…
Away! Away on fairy light,
Tomorrow bound this
Sapphire night…

Die not your dreams maiden fair,
On unfurled wings where fairies dare…
Weep no more on downcast eyes,
Away! Away where
Fairies fly…

Immortal light of moon forlorn,
Dreams fair the maid her
Wishes born…

20

May my faith always be at the end of day, like a hummingbird ...returning to its favorite flower...

Sanober Khan

"The Hummingbird"

The mountains I become part of it, the herbs, the fir tree, I become part of it…
the morning mist, the clouds, the gathering waters….I become part of it…
-Navajo Chant

Yonder flies a hummingbird waiting evening's hour,
Flaunting wings of crimson red from flower to flower…
Upward springing, purpl'd breast, on stems of slender green,
By modest weeds unnamed or known,
In woodlands seldom seen…

In evenings quiet sonnet, 'neath skyways turquoise-blue,
By forests fragrant bodice in twilight's early dew…
As yonder flies a hummingbird in woodlands seldom seen,
Upward springing, purpl'd breast, on
Stems of slender green…

Curtains close on western skies while bidding day adieu,
As yonder flies a hummingbird 'neath skyways turquoise-blue…
In evenings quiet sonnet waiting evening's hour,
Flaunting wings of crimson red
From flower to flower…

While humble flowers in disguise sleep in woodland's bed,
Yonder flies a hummingbird with
Wings of crimson-red…

22

If you talk to the animals, they will talk with you and you will know each other. If you do not talk to them, you will not know them and what you do not know, you will fear...what one fears, one destroys...

Chief Dan George

"The Spirit's Ride"

Out of the earth I sing for them, a horse nation, I sing for them. Out of
the earth, I sing for them…the animals I sing for them…
-Teton Sioux Chant

Sing the songs in speechless trance,
O'er sage of prairies purple dance…
Echo's there midst scattered light,
Beats leathered drum in
Pale of night…

Shadowed there by mustangs side,
With feathered lance, the spirits ride…
Flying mane their nostrils flare,
Astride their mounts no
Mortals dare…

Dance of ghosts each twilight sings,
Wolf'n howls as eagle's wing…
Lance to lance on horse astride,
Spirits they on mustangs
Ride…

Descending slow midst scattered light,
Beats leathered drum in pale of night…
Shadowed there by mustangs side,
With feathered lance the
Spirit's ride…

I shall be telling this with a sigh, somewhere ages and ages hence; two roads diverged in a wood, and I, I took the one less traveled by...and that has made all the difference...

Robert Frost

"The Well-Worn Stair"

*We've all got both light and dark inside us. What matters is the part
we choose to act on… that's who we really are…*
-J.K. Rowling

Not here but there I take the stair,
Up yonder hill, I know not where…
Nightingales in murmured prose,
Sing mingled notes by
Scented rose…

Tentative steps to my dismay,
Soft worn the path I walk today…
Clouds beckon me "take the stair",
Up yonder hill I know
Not where…

Nightingales they sing their songs,
Their murmured prose of right and wrong…
Bowed head in doubt I must delay,
Past scented rose I walk
Away…

Oh so gently tread the stair,
By scented rose in fragrant air…
On soft worn pathways walked today,
Or bow your head and
Walk away…

Beware! Beware the well-worn stair

G. NYSTROM. 18

As you walk upon the sacred earth, treat each step as a prayer...

Black Elk

"What Time Forgot"

Wilderness is the preservation of the World...
-Henry David Thoreau

Whispered winds in sad dismay,
Through forest trees in quiet sway...
Hearing not the wolve'n howl,
Or feeling not a coyote's
Prowl...

Spreads meadows soft in silent view,
No flowers there once white and blue...
Fall of snow or spring yet seen,
No sparrows fly in forest
Green...

Woeful winds echo not,
Wolve'n howls time forgot...
Viewless there as eagles wing,
In quiet sway the
Evergreen...

No flowers there once white and blue,
In valleys deep time once knew...
Fall of cones forget them not,
The wolve'n howls time
Forgot...

Rivers dammed no longer flow,
No coyotes prowl, no flowers
Grow...

The world is not to be put in order. The world is order, incarnate. It is for us to put ourselves in unison with this order…

Henry Miller

"WHEN CATTAILS DIE"

We do not inherit the Earth from our ancestors, we borrow it from our children…
-Native American Quote

Bloom no more the cattails in a pond without a shore,
Golden is the meadow where flowers grew before….
Strains of silence beckon in once this dell of dew,
Scattered lifeless lilies not colored
White or blue…

Once among the flowers named but weeds unknown,
Danced flies of butter gaily where cattails there had grown….
Silver was the moonlight o'er meadow and beyond,
Sang frogs in bullish cadence in once
Their happy pond…

There beyond tomorrow where bees of honey flew,
Fragrant they the flowers while waving cattails grew…
Speckled moonlight twinkled in nightly disarray,
As frogs in bullish cadence sang
Each twilight's gray…

Bloom no more the cattails where could they all have gone?
Twinkles not the moonlight awaiting sad each dawn…
Weeds unknown as flowers fragrant not the shore,
No frogs in bullish cadence sing where
They did before…

Scenting not the flowers cries the butterfly,
Away from home now searching when
Ponds and cattails die…

30

In joined hands, there is still some token of hope…in clenched fist…none…

Victor Hugo

"When I Die"

There is a pleasure in the pathless woods, there is rapture on the lonely shore, there is society, where none intrudes, by the deep sea, and music in its roar; I love not man the less, but Nature more…
-Lord Byron

When I die I want to live
In a place where peace abounds…
With no more war and killing,
Where joy and hope
Are found…

I want to hear a howling wolf,
Howl beneath the moon…
I want to hear the oceans
From a clean and
Sandy dune…

When I die I want to live,
Where creatures still roam free…
While walking with the lions.
And tigers walk
With me…

I want to taste a river,
Un-damned and left to flow…
As I see the tree lined valleys,
Where tiny blue-bells
Grow…

I want to hear a raindrop,
As it falls into the sea…
A sound so loud it echoes,
It's message back
To me…

When I die I want to live,
Where everyone is free…
With no more hate and killing,
A place for you
And me…

Far away there in the sunshine are my brightest aspirations. I may not reach them, but I can look up and see their beauty, believe in them, and try to follow where they lead…

Louisa May Alcott

"When Starlight Falls"

Dreams are wishes with wings…
-Melody Hamby Goss

Adorn me not from afar,
Midst a storm of falling stars…
Golden glittered sights and sounds,
Starlight pale in dreams
Abound…

Divine the mist in heaven there,
Fairies winged in fragrant air…
Pleasing notes as cherubs sing,
Echoes there on fairies
Wings…

Wake me not from dreaming nigh,
In golden starlight as I fly…
Gathered there winged fairies all,
Midst a storm when starlight
Falls…

Dwelling not in mortals sky,
Dreaming dreams as fairies fly…
Golden glittered falling stars,
Embrace me there from
Afar…

Eyes wide-shut my wishes dare,
With fairies winged in
Fragrant air…

The Gods know what it is to be eternal, and they love to toy with mortals who use absolutes…

Josephine Angelini

"Where Ravens Fly"

(Thor)

*Nevermore shall men make slaves of others! Not in Asgard – not on Earth – not anyplace where
the hammer of Thor can be swung – or where men of good faith hold freedom dear…*
-Stan Lee

Dark of world no earth nor sky,
A murky world where ravens fly…
Embers burn upon the sea,
Sails his ship, mates
And he…

O'er the mast ravens there,
To Thor they call…"Beware, Beware"
Aflame the seas no earth no sky,
This murky world where
Ravens fly…

A league, a league set the sails,
Angry waves and roaring wails…
A'light his sword helm in hand,
Thunder there spies now
The land…

Sea-waves crash upon the shore,
Sails his ship forevermore…
O'er the mast ravens there,
To Thor they call,
"Beware, Beware…"

When the owl sings the night is silent...

Charles de Leusse

"With Winking Eye"

Every night the owl with his wild monkey-face calls through the black branches, and
the mice freeze and rabbits shiver in the snowy fields – and then there is the long,
deep trough of silence when he stops singing, and steps into the air...
-Mary Oliver

O'er woodlands modest evening guise,
Awakes the owl at moonlight's rise...
Warbles not to silvered sky,
Hoots the owl with
Winking eye...

On viewless wings with quiet breath,
Strays a mouse to easeful death...
From his bough in silvered sky,
Hoots the owl with
Winking eye...

Light-winged there his kingdom home,
On floor of forest shadows roam...
Faint of morn 'neath silvered sky,
Hoots the owl with
Sleepy eye...

On forest floor no mice at play,
When hoots the owl
Another day...

We ought to do good to others as simply as a horse runs, or a bee makes honey, or a vine bears grapes season after season without thinking of the grapes it has borne…

Marcus Aurelius

"Of Wisteria & Lavender"

I will be the gladdest thing under the sun! I will touch a hundred flowers and not pick one…
-Edna St. Vincent Millay

Purple fragrant petals on trellis painted white,
Forever scenting summer to bumblebee's delight…
By tiny fairies winging o'er my greening lawn,
Leaving little prints of silver in
Morning's quiet dawn…

Dreary midnight wanders away in pinkish rays,
On shadows of wisteria in morning's early grays…
Her purple fragrant petals, on trellis painted white,
Waves to lavender and violets to
Bumblebees delight…

Budding roses scarlet where flies of butter dance,
By lightly painted lattice as dragonflies romance…
Speckled sunbeams playing over greening lawn,
Shading tiny fairies in morning's
Quiet dawn…

Wisteria and Lavender o'er morning lawn's and lea,
Forever scenting summer to delight'd
Bumblebees…

40

Printed in the United States
By Bookmasters